ENGINEERED BY NATURE

MOUNT EVEREST

BY MARTHA LONDON

CONTENT CONSULTANT
MICHAEL MURPHY, PHD
PROFESSOR
DEPARTMENT OF EARTH AND ATMOSPHERIC SCIENCES
UNIVERSITY OF HOUSTON

Kids Core
An Imprint of Abdo Publishing
abdobooks.com

abdobooks.com

Published by Abdo Publishing, a division of ABDO, PO Box 398166, Minneapolis, Minnesota 55439. Copyright © 2021 by Abdo Consulting Group, Inc. International copyrights reserved in all countries. No part of this book may be reproduced in any form without written permission from the publisher. Kids Core™ is a trademark and logo of Abdo Publishing.

Printed in the United States of America, North Mankato, Minnesota
022020
092020

Cover Photo: Shutterstock Images
Interior Photos: Zhosan Olexandr/Shutterstock Images, 4–5; Gesman Tamang/AFP/Getty Images, 6; iStockphoto, 9, 26; Shutterstock Images, 10, 15, 20–21, 22, 28; Daniel Prudek/Shutterstock Images, 12–13; Travel Stock/Shutterstock Images, 17; Phunjo Lama/AFP/Getty Images, 18; Niranjan Shrestha/AP Images, 25; Red Line Editorial, 28–29

Editor: Marie Pearson
Series Designer: Megan Ellis

Library of Congress Control Number: 2019954089

Publisher's Cataloging-in-Publication Data

Names: London, Martha, author.
Title: Mount Everest / by Martha London
Description: Minneapolis, Minnesota : Abdo Publishing, 2021 | Series: Engineered by nature | Includes online resources and index.
Identifiers: ISBN 9781532192890 (lib. bdg.) | ISBN 9781098210793 (ebook)
Subjects: LCSH: Everest, Mount (China and Nepal)--Juvenile literature. | Natural monuments--Juvenile literature. | Mountain peaks--Juvenile literature. | National parks and reserves--Juvenile literature. | Landforms--Juvenile literature.
Classification: DDC 910.202--dc23

CONTENTS

Climbers and local guides carry camping gear up Mount Everest.

CHAPTER 1

JOURNEY TO THE TOP

Climbers and local guides set up tents on Mount Everest. Before continuing up the mountain, the climbers need to rest. The air has less **oxygen** up here. Climbers can get sick if they climb too quickly. Their bodies have to get used to the higher **elevation**.

Climbing Mount Everest is very dangerous.

There are four major camps on Everest. After Camp 3, the air is too thin for humans to stay very long.

Each climber wears boots with sharp metal spikes on the bottom. The spikes dig into the snow and ice. Climbers place their feet carefully. There are places where the snow and ice drop into deep cracks.

Near the top of the mountain, climbers use ropes to scale the steep sides. Climbing Mount Everest is a goal for many experienced climbers. It takes years of training. The mountain challenges even the most skilled climbers.

Most Climbs

Nepali mountain guide Kami Rita reached the peak for the twenty-fourth time in 2019. That is the most times anyone has gone to the **summit**.

Tallest Mountain

Mount Everest's summit is 29,035 feet (8,850 m) above sea level. The peak is part of a mountain range called the Himalayas. Mount Everest is in Asia. It is on the border between Nepal and a region in China called Tibet.

Its high elevation means snow and ice are present all year. High winds and cold temperatures make the top of the mountain dangerous. Winds can reach 100 miles per hour (160 km/h). Temperatures can be as cold as -76 degrees Fahrenheit (-60°C).

The Himalayas are a huge mountain range.

Some people visit Mount Everest but do not climb the mountain.

The top of the mountain has just one-third of the oxygen that exists at sea level. Climbers carry tanks of oxygen. With oxygen, they can stay at the summit safely.

Mount Everest is the shape of a three-sided pyramid. Its fame draws people from all over the world. It took millions of years to form. It is a beautiful and dangerous place.

Climbing Mount Everest is a challenge. Mountain climber Cory Richards says:

> It's still as high, cold, and formidable as it ever was. How one chooses to climb it is as much a reflection of creativity as skill.

Source: Freddie Wilkinson. "Want to Climb Mount Everest?" *National Geographic*, 22 Jan. 2019, nationalgeographic.com. Accessed 24 Oct. 2019.

Comparing Texts

Think about the quote. Does it support the information in this chapter? Or does it give a different perspective? Explain how in a few sentences.

Mount Everest and the surrounding Himalayan mountains formed because of Earth's movement.

CHAPTER 2

GROWING SLOWLY

Mount Everest formed as land shifted over time. Earth's surface is made up of large pieces of rock. These pieces are called tectonic plates. Tectonic plates make up the ocean floor and continents.

The plates are always moving. Sometimes they run into one another. Between 40 million and 50 million years ago, two plates collided. One plate pushed up over the other. This event took millions of years. The force of the plates hitting each other began to form the Himalayas. Mount Everest began forming 2.6 million years ago. The plates are still pushing against each other.

What's in a Name?

The Tibetan name for Mount Everest, *Chomolungma*, means "Goddess Mother of the World." Surveyor Andrew Waugh named Mount Everest after surveyor George Everest. Everest created ways to find certain points of land. In 1856, Waugh used Everest's methods to find the location of the mountain's peak.

Moving Plates

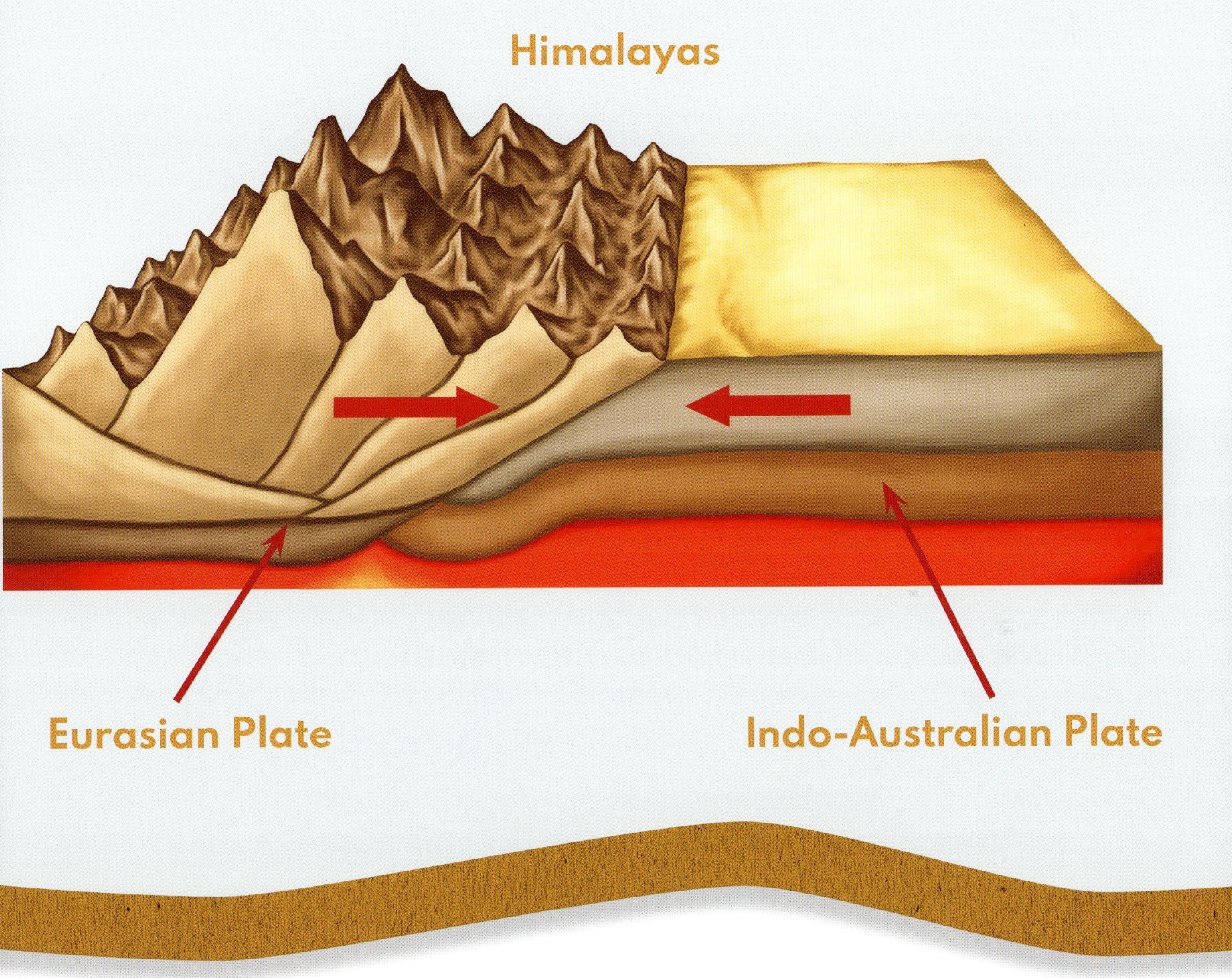

This graphic shows how Mount Everest formed. The Himalayas are part of the Eurasian plate. The plate is pushed up by the Indo-Australian plate as they hit each other.

Life on the Mountain

Plants and animals have lived on and near Mount Everest since it started forming. But they cannot survive at the top of the mountain. There is not enough oxygen. People, plants, and animals do live up to 16,000 feet (4,800 m) on the mountain.

Sherpa people from Tibet and Nepal began living near Everest hundreds of years ago. The people traveled around the mountain. They grew crops, and their animals grazed.

Nepali and Tibetan people see Everest as holy. Many people who live near Everest do not climb the mountain. Climbing it is dangerous. Sherpas are one of the few groups who do.

Some Sherpa people live in villages near Mount Everest.

Western climbers began coming to the mountain in the 1900s. Sherpa guides helped them climb.

Sherpa guides face many dangers when climbing Everest.

Being a guide on Everest is dangerous. **Blizzards** and **avalanches** are common. These events can be deadly. The mountain has loose rocks. There are deep canyons in the ice. But Nepali and Tibetan people still lead visitors up Everest. They make more money as guides than they would as farmers.

Explore Online

Look at the website below. Does it give any new evidence to support Chapter Two?

Where Is the Highest Mountain?

abdocorelibrary.com/mount-everest

As humans visit Mount Everest,
they leave behind trash.

CHAPTER 3

A CHANGING MOUNTAIN

Mount Everest is so big that it is hard to tell it's moving. But as tectonic plates move, so does the mountain. Even the height of Everest is changing. Not all of the changes on the mountain are natural, though. Humans have a big effect on Everest.

Mount Everest is moving, but it's too slow for the human eye to see.

Mount Everest moves northeastward. Scientists estimate that each year Everest shifts a fraction of an inch. Scientists also believe that Everest is getting taller. They estimate Everest grows less than 1 inch (2.5 cm) each year.

Human Effects

Everest is changing in many ways. Humans are part of the reason the mountain is changing. More people climb Everest each year. But there are few bathrooms or trash cans. That means a lot of trash is left on the mountain.

Trash Mountain

Mount Everest is covered in more than 200,000 pounds (91,000 kg) of trash. Melted snow washes trash into streams. The trash can make people in villages sick. People in Nepal and Tibet are working to clean the mountain. Groups of climbers bring trash off the mountain.

Many climbers dump their empty oxygen tanks at the summit. They do not want to carry the weight back down.

The trash washes into waterways when snow and ice melt. It **pollutes** drinking water for villages. Groups are working to clean the trash on the mountain. But it takes a long time.

Everest is becoming more dangerous with climate change. Climate change is causing Earth to get warmer. Gases in the sky trap heat. They keep Earth warm. Cars and factories add more gases to the air. This makes Earth warmer.

Climate change is causing **glaciers** to melt on Everest. The rock high on the mountain is held together with ice. As the ice melts, the rock

Nepal is working to clean up the growing amount of waste on the mountain.

becomes unstable. Falling ice and rocks could become more common. A warming climate means climbers will have to find different paths up the mountain.

It is important to protect Mount Everest and the surrounding area. Then people in the future can still enjoy it.

People want to climb Mount Everest because it is a challenge. The mountain continues to change. It is people's job to care for the mountain.

Duncan Quincey is a science professor. He spoke about Everest's melting glaciers:

> These glaciers are changing. They're changing very rapidly . . . and our best evidence supports the fact that it's [driven by climate].

Source: Sarah Kaplan. "Lakes Are Forming on Top of Mount Everest's Glaciers." *Washington Post*, 30 Nov. 2015, washingtonpost.com. Accessed 24 Oct. 2019.

Point of View

What is the author's point of view on Everest's melting glaciers? What is your point of view? Write a short essay about how they are similar and different.

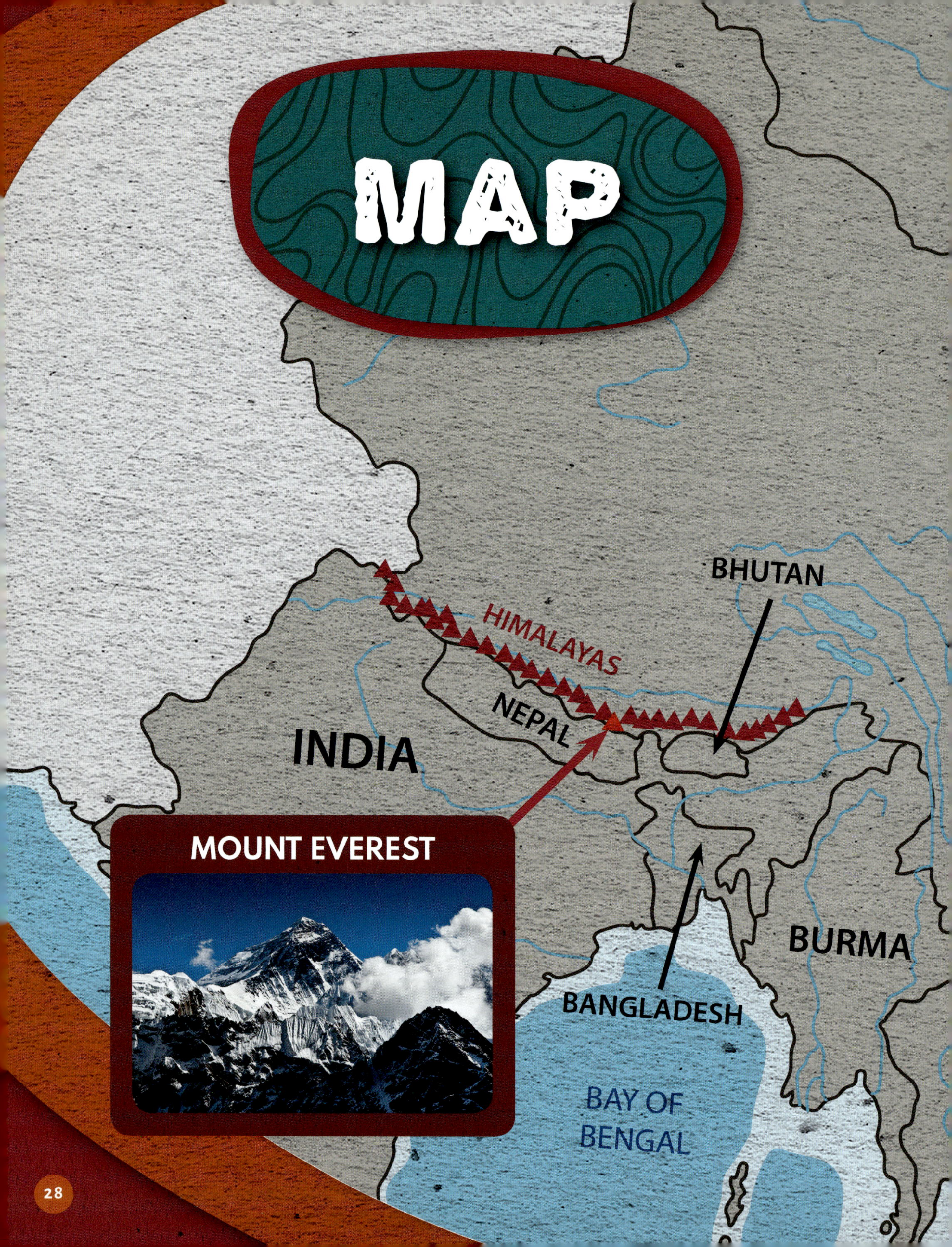

MAP
BHUTAN
HIMALAYAS
NEPAL
INDIA
MOUNT EVEREST
BURMA
BANGLADESH
BAY OF
BENGAL

MONGOLIA
CHINA
• Mount Everest began forming into its present shape 2.6 million years ago.
• It is the highest point on Earth. It stands 29,035 feet (8,850 m) above sea level.
N
W
E
S

Glossary

avalanches
events when snow breaks loose from the side of a mountain and slides down, burying things in the snow's path

blizzards
storms when strong winds make it hard to see by causing snow to swirl around

elevation
the height of something compared to sea level

glaciers
large sheets of ice that stay frozen all year

oxygen
a gas in the air that most animals need to breathe or absorb

pollutes
makes something dirty

summit
the highest point on a mountain

Online Resources

To learn more about Mount Everest, visit our free resource websites below.

Visit **abdocorelibrary.com** or scan this QR code for free Common Core resources for teachers and students, including vetted activities, multimedia, and booklinks, for deeper subject comprehension.

Visit **abdobooklinks.com** or scan this QR code for free additional online weblinks for further learning. These links are routinely monitored and updated to provide the most current information available.

Learn More

Herman, Gail. *Climbing Everest.* Random House, 2015.

Medina, Nico. *Where Is Mount Everest?* Penguin, 2015.

Vanden Branden, Claire. *Asia.* Abdo Publishing, 2019.

Index

About the Author

Martha London writes books for young readers full-time. When she isn't writing, you can find her hiking in the woods.